I0712024

AUXILIARY AUTHORITIES

The way to really improve México

AUXILIARY AUTHORITIES

The way to really improve México

LIC. COSME SANTOVEÑA VELÁZQUEZ

DEDICATION

I want to dedicate this book to my mother R.I.P.D. Mainly, since she was the one who taught me day by day to try to improve my environment, to love my country, to help people who did not have the same opportunities that I had, to work hard every day, to be positive, to participate, to pick up that piece of paper thrown in the street, to always put a grain of sand to improve people's lives, even if I didn't know them.

I also dedicate it to my sisters and my nephews that I love so much, and I hope that I can contribute a little of my knowledge and experiences as an auxiliary authority, so that they continue to be better people than they already are, and that, as my mother taught us , keep trying to contribute that grain of sand to society every day, to improve our home, our street, our neighborhood, our municipality, our state, our country, and our world.

I also dedicate it to my father, grandmothers, grandfathers, uncles, aunts, cousins, cousins and all my family, friends and neighbors, (sorry for not naming them all, but thank God there are many and the list would be very long) and also to my ex-girlfriend, (which by the way I apologize for all these years, that because I was working I neglected her a little), but let her know that it was for work, (not for anything else), and even so I still love her very much.

I hope you like it.

CONTENTS

THANKS

First of all, I want to thank God for giving me all the necessary elements and experiences to be able to write this book that had been pending for many years, and only until now was I able to do it.

Also, to my mother that I know, that, from heaven, I am only her pen to be able to capture through this book, all that affection for Mexico that she loved so much, and so much wanted to help and always improve.

LOVE YOU

INTRODUCTION

Has it happened to you that when you leave your house very positive and motivated, but along the way to your work or school suddenly without realizing it, little by little you complain about the potholes, the sidewalks (if there are any), from stray dogs, from unmaintained parks and gardens, from floods, from dirty streets, from traffic, or unpaved streets, etc. If so, then allow me to share with you in the simplest way possible, a bit of my experience throughout all those years that I had the opportunity to be an auxiliary authority, so that you are encouraged (regardless of how old you are), and Let's get our batteries together, and try to participate to improve a little more, our communities and our country.

 I was a normal citizen studying for a degree in administration, working in the family business and also thanks to my mother and my school I had the opportunity to travel to one or another country, and every day I walked through my community or other communities, I went to the store to buy something, I went to the park, the mall, etc. Suddenly the image of those beautiful countries that I visited came to mind, and when I looked around me, usually and even though I didn't want to, I saw something that wasn't working, something was almost always wrong, (some little detail) either the potholes in the streets, the sidewalks in poor condition, the traffic light did not work, the public lighting was out, the park full of loose dogs and poop everywhere, the uncut grass in the parks, there were never police or they were sleeping, the noisy neighbor, littering, water leaks, etc.

I always saw politicians on television and their promising
campaigns, but in the end my community never advanced,
(which was one of the beautiful ones), but it was always the
same, as if time did not pass through my community.

(Even my maternal grandfather, RIP, when suddenly, after a
long time, they covered a pothole, he cried as a joke because
he said that he had been living with them for years, and he saw
them grow from when they were little until they became big,
that he loved them as if they were their children).

I am one of those people who did not like to be just a spectator, but wanted to be an actor, and I felt that desire to participate and do something to improve my community, and directly impact with my actions, (without being municipal president or governor), I wanted people to reflect, but I didn't know how to do it, or where to start, until one day I saw a call posted (hidden, so that no one would see it) in the park to participate as a municipal delegate or auxiliary authority, (I had no idea what that was, nor was there much information), and in the year 2000, for the first time, in my case I had the opportunity to participate as a municipal delegate in my community, and it was that time that I discovered how a municipality works (city hall in cdmx), but at the same time I realized that hardly anyone does anything to improve their environment because we are all very busy with our personal things, and we want to leave everything to the authorities, and the authorities usually p They think that everything is perfect around them, because hardly anyone complains or asks them for anything.

And so a vicious circle is created, where the end result is what we currently live in, which is why I decided to write this book for auxiliary authorities, and thus contribute my grain of sand to this great country that I love so much, and of course the objective is to motivate more people throughout Mexico to participate and reflect to be auxiliary authorities and overcome that fear or those doubts about how to help, and really begin to improve their community.

What will also be of great help to the municipal presidents and mayors, to facilitate and explain in a simple way the great work that the auxiliary authorities in the municipalities and mayors have, and in this way work as a team for the good of our beloved Mexico.

WHAT IS AN AUXILIARY AUTHORITY?

I am going to try to explain it in a simple way, since the auxiliary authorities as we currently know them have existed for many years, but over the years, the name has been changing, and even now it can have several names depending on your community, but normally they are those neighbors who are really on the court, on the battlefield, they are the ones who live the real problems day by day of their community to which they belong, and normally we know them as delegates, sub-delegates, heads of apple, heads of barracks, etc.

You can or can name them in different ways, but in general they are women and men elected by their community or by the city council, they must be of legal age, and who participate in improving their neighborhood, neighborhood, town, etc. to help maintain order, cleanliness, tranquility, social peace, security, the protection of neighbors, the safety of animals, as well as to promote citizen participation among the residents of their community.

In short, they are those neighbors who are chartered and who are always looking at how they can improve their community and not just their house. And that many times we ignore them, despise them or even tell them "they are the ones who have nothing to do".

In my case, I ran into some people (of those who complicate everything), who discussed whether the name of "alternate delegate" is actually that of "sub-delegate", or if it is a separate figure, etc.

I believe that the name or names that we give to this function do not matter so much, nor is it the intention of this book, I believe that what is really important is that these people be valued, and above all to make known that it exists in the municipalities this support figure called "auxiliary authority", in which you can participate directly, to really improve your community, and for that I have written this book.

WHAT REQUIREMENTS DO I NEED TO PARTICIPATE AS AN AUXILIARY AUTHORITY IN MY COMMUNITY?

The requirements are very simple, usually in all the municipalities of Mexico (2,471 municipalities) and (16 mayors in CDMX), they ask you to be:
- Mexican by birth
- Adult
- No criminal record
- Reside in that community for a minimum time
- Voting license.
- etc.

In some cases there are auxiliary authorities that have no studies or very few studies. there are even some with a bachelor's degree (as in my case), and although it is not a requirement to have a certain degree of studies, sometimes there is the eternal debate of whether the authorities assistants should be people with a certain level of education, or that doesn't matter, the important thing is that they want to participate.

QUESTIONS TO REFLECT ON:

What do you think is correct, whether or not they have studies?

Do you know the auxiliary authority of your community?

Do you think it is important that auxiliary authorities have a certain age, in order to make better decisions for your community?

Currently the auxiliary authorities do not receive any salary, this is called an "HONORIFIC" position, but they have a little support with the collection of some types of certificates that they issue. (although I never charge anything to my neighbors) The truth is that sometimes you end up putting money from your pocket and with some other mentioned.
But in the end, the experience and learning are worth it.
In some entities, legislation is being legislated so that the auxiliary authorities receive some type of diet or salary, but well, up to now they still do not receive any payment.

Although personally, on the one hand I think that financial support is necessary, because sometimes there are a lot of expenses, but on the other hand I think that the position of auxiliary authority is a way of discovering the true neighbors who are born leaders, because Although they do not receive a salary, they always do everything possible to improve their community. And I think that, if they received a payment, they would already do it for the interest of the money and not for the interest of really improving their environment.

QUESTIONS TO REFLECT ON:

What do you think, should the auxiliary authorities receive financial support or not?

Do you think that, if they received support, they would do it with the same passion that the current ones do?

CAN ANYONE BE AN AUXILIARY AUTHORITY?

Actually, anyone who meets the above requirements could be an auxiliary authority, the problem is that many people participate, thinking that they are going to get rich, or because they have the pure appointment of being the "community delegate".
And things don't work like that, there really are people who love to manage, and improve our community without expecting anything in return, other than the benefit of what is managed itself, but there are also many people who hate managing something, because the neighbor that they like is also going to benefit from what he manages, so it is better not to manage anything, so as not to benefit anyone who dislikes us.

Which of the two types of people are you?

Recently I had to see an election of municipal delegates in a municipality, and a lady, who was the most troublesome, (who had never been a delegate), did everything possible to remain as a proprietary delegate, and when people asked her why What did she want to be a proprietary delegate? If she didn't have the time to manage, what better could she enter as a substitute delegate to see how it worked? In the end, she remained as the proprietary delegate.
After a while I returned to that community, and I found out that this person never has time and has not done anything or managed anything. (we already knew since the election)

In my opinion, I think it's not bad to want to participate to see what it's all about, but for that there are substitute delegates, and she was able to remain as substitute and accompany the owners to the negotiations, and later in the next election, she you could decide whether or not you like to go manage and re-engage.

WHAT IS THE USE OF BEING AN AUXILIARY AUTHORITY?

Many people believe that it is useless and that they are just free problems, but in my experience, it helped me to know and understand how the environment works in my municipality, in my state and therefore in my country. Just as I learned how to manage and obtain many things that were lacking in my community or how to improve services, I also met many of my neighbors and their ways of thinking, I met and interacted with some politicians, I even went out on a interview on local television with the fire commander.
Currently I am also the president of an Association of settlers, but having been a municipal delegate opened the doors for me to be able to have this position, and continue helping more people in any municipality that I find in Mexico.

Some neighbors even asked me, I don't know why you like to get into trouble? that they wanted to go live in another country (they don't know what it's like to live in another country), or how bad the current government was, or if it was because of "X" party or person, etc.
Other people even told me that the municipal president was there for that, that we paid him for that, so that he would solve the problems of the municipality. But precisely one of the reasons for the existence of the auxiliary authority is to work as a team with the city council, since they do not know everything that happens in your community, and for that you are an auxiliary authority, to "help" them in informing and managing the needs of your community.

In short, everything and everyone was wrong, but they were the only ones who were always right and, according to them, they always have the best ideas (but they never expose them, nor do they say them to apply them).

And when I asked them, what have you done to improve your community? They always told me "I pay my taxes when I buy my cigarettes and soft drinks at the store".

That's where I also realized that people believe that just by buying things in the store, all the problems in the community will be solved out of the blue.

I believe that in order to aspire to become the most perfect community possible, it must include: sidewalks in good condition and wide, good streets, good public lighting, signs, that there is order in the neighborhood, that they are clean, that there are

the necessary services to be able to live comfortably, that there is security and tranquility in your community, in short, small great details that will make us all live better.

And the best of all is that all this is possible, with your efforts

and new ideas that you can contribute as an auxiliary authority.

A friend who lives in a luxury condominium one day asked me, do you think that, with beautiful sidewalks, pretty streets and little flowers, you are already going to be the perfect community? It takes more than that to be perfect, he told me; (and he is very right), but I also believe that if we at least start with the basic things that any community should have, (because there are many communities in Mexico that have no electricity, no sidewalks, no drainage, no internet, no bus stops, or water, etc.) if we managed at least those basic things, I think we would make things easier for all of us to get ahead.

QUESTIONS TO REFLECT ON:

Do you think that the steps that the auxiliary authority of your community can take before the town hall really work, to help you live better?

What other things do you think your community needs, to become the perfect community?

Do you think that the perfect community, or almost perfect, can exist?

What community in Mexico or in the world do you think is the perfect community?

Do you think someone can think about arts, science or philosophy, if they don't even have water to flush the bathroom, or wash the dishes, wash clothes, or don't have electricity?

CAN I BE AN AUXILIARY AUTHORITY IF I LIVE IN A CONDOMINIUM?

Currently that is a big question from many people, that is why I decided to include this question, since there are currently many horizontal and vertical condominiums, which are within a neighborhood, subdivision, town, etc.
If you live in the condominium, and you want to participate as an auxiliary authority of your neighborhood, you can do it, but if you win along with your return, then you will be appointed by the city council and at that moment you will have to be the auxiliary authority and see to all the problems. of your neighborhood, not just those of your condominium. (you have to see all the topics of the municipal side)

In a neighborhood there can be several condominiums, and the delegate or auxiliary authority is the representative before the city council of all those condominiums, subdivision, ejido, etc. As long as they are all within the same neighborhood or community they represent.

In some cases, the communities are so large that only one auxiliary authority is not enough to manage all the problems of its community, at that moment it is when the creation of a sub-delegation or even a new delegation must be managed so that they have their authority. assistant who represents that area that was not covered by the previous delegation.

Your condominium, regardless of all the others, must have a general assembly to appoint its board of directors, where they will elect a president, a secretary and a treasurer and their members.

In my case, when I saw the call, I had to bring together 3 people who were proprietary delegates with their respective 3 substitute delegates, and what normally happens, no one wanted to participate, because no one had time, no one wanted problems, no money was earned, etc..
But with a lot of convincing work, in the end some older people in my community gave me their trust and support and I was able to make my form to be able to participate.

Currently the rules have changed a bit, and now you must include 50% women and 50% men when integrating your payroll for the issue of gender equality, which I think is very good, because it encourages women to participate in problems and solutions in your community.

In some communities, it is worth mentioning that the way of designating a list can vary, since they choose them at the moment, among the people who are present, and want to participate.

HOW IS THE AUXILIARY AUTHORITY OF MY COMMUNITY CHOSEN?

I remember that time posters were put up in the neighborhood stores, in some houses, etc., announcing the different forms that had registered to participate, and the dates on which the elections would take place, and we visited house by house proposing our work plan to improve our community.

Which was very interesting, because I discovered all the new ideas to improve our neighborhood, and I also learned about the problems and solutions that each neighbor had.

On voting day, booths were set up in the park, and with a representative from each slate present, and city hall staff to attest that everything was carried out according to the call, at the end of the day the votes were counted, and the slate with the most votes was the one that would stay for the next three years. In some communities of some municipalities, I still had to see that what they call uses and customs are used, and those who want to vote for form "X" are placed on the right side, and those who want to vote for form "Y" are put on the left side...

The truth is that I don't think it's the best way to do it, because the vote must be free and secret, and that day in that community they yelled at everything (traitors, on this side we're also going to give pantries, I'm going to tell your compadre that you left with those from the other list, etc....) It was very interesting to see how in some places of our beloved Mexico, they are still far behind in that aspect, but that is the purpose of this guide, that together we build better communities, more democratic, and with greater citizen participation.

Personally, I think it helps a lot, because you learn how the municipalities work (town hall in CDMX), and the municipalities form the states and the states make the country.

It also gives you the opportunity to get to know and interact with people, and for them to get to know how you work, that you are honest, that you are responsible, that you are really interested in seeing how you can solve their problems, etc.

In general, you make a political career from below and I think that many current politicians that we have, if they had been auxiliary authorities from the beginning, would have helped them a lot in their management work and climb politically correctly.

HOW DO I KNOW, WHAT ARE MY FUNCTIONS AS AN AUXILIARY AUTHORITY?

Do not worry if at first you do not know what it is about or how you are going to do it, because normally when you are elected as a delegate or auxiliary authority in your community, the city council in turn invites all the elected delegates to take a protest, and they give your appointment, your seal, they give you your current municipal edict, your regulations for municipal delegates or auxiliary authorities, and sometimes the municipal organic law of your state, etc... They give you everything you need to know, and they guide you so that you can carry out your functions correctly.

In general, you are going to learn little by little, how the work of auxiliary authority works, do not be discouraged that nobody is born knowing everything, but the important thing is that you want to learn, participate and support the improvement of your community, and if we do so all the communities, we will soon see a better country.

WHAT IS THE MUNICIPAL BAND?

The municipal decree is the main legal system (a small book), which works as if it were the constitution in each municipality, which is published every February 5, there are many interesting things about your municipality. Its history, its anthem, how your municipality is organized territorially, the population, tells you who governs in that period, the administrative offenses (what you cannot do) and their sanctions, etc.

It can be said that it is the book of the rules of the game in each municipality. If they don't give it to you, you can download it on your municipality's website, and you also help to cut down fewer trees. In the special case of Mexico City, they call it a government program. (although it is different). When I was an auxiliary authority, I asked some neighbors if they knew what the Municipal Bando was, and some of them answered yes, that they had come to play at the park some years ago.

That's where I realized that people in general have no idea what the municipal decree is, nor who publishes it, nor where it is published.

This book is modified every year by the municipal president, together with the aldermen, and articles are added or removed according to the needs of each community. (you can suggest that they put or modify articles)

I think that if each person knew the municipal faction of their municipality, it would help all of us to live more organized, and without fewer lawsuits. Because I see it as if it were a game that we all play, but almost no one knows the rules of the game. (then imagine the relaxation that there is in a game, where nobody knows the rules).

There are even people who asked me, what was the use of them knowing the municipal side?

DO I HAVE TO BELONG TO ANY POLITICAL PARTY TO PARTICIPATE AS AN AUXILIARY AUTHORITY?

Normally people think that to participate as a delegate or auxiliary authority you must belong to the same political party that was elected in your municipality, but the truth is that No, since anyone can participate from whatever party, since the needs of all neighbors are the same, regardless of party, they all need good sidewalks, good streets, public lighting, security in their streets, houses, etc.

And at the moment that you are already democratically elected and they give you your appointment as "Auxiliary Authority", at that moment you must understand that the time for elections is over, and that it is time to get to work for the good of all those who live in your community, without party colors, or resentments, remember that the goal is to improve your community.

HOW OFTEN DO THE AUXILIARY AUTHORITIES CHANGE?

Usually they are every three years, it is the time that each council lasts, but in some communities, it can vary. But ideally, it should be every 3 years, so that everyone has the opportunity to participate.

Normally when a proprietary delegate finishes his term, he can no longer be re-elected for the same position, and the one who is his substitute is now the one who is proposed for proprietary delegate and that is how it works, the problem is that later there are communities that have been doing This for many years, for example, when I participated for the first time, the delegate and her husband from my community had been in the same position for about 15 years.

So in one call she participated, and in the other her husband, and so they changed positions for more than 15 years, arguing that nobody wants to participate, then again they were left.

QUESTIONS TO REFLECT ON:

Do you think it's healthy for a couple to last so many years in the same position?

Do you think people don't want to participate, or don't really realize that they can participate?

IS THE AUXILIARY AUTHORITY RESPONSIBLE FOR THE COMMUNITY'S WATER WELL?

Normally all communities have two ways of having water, either the well is owned by the town hall, or owned by the community, and if it is owned by the community, a "water committee" is formed with the neighbors, who manage the well.

Personally, I have had the experience of seeing how both forms of administration work, but I have seen that when there are water committees, the neighbors almost kill each other, because some do not pay, others do not want to pay so much, another owes the compadre about the goddaughter's party, and that's why he doesn't pay her, in short, many problems arise when the community's water well is managed by a committee, and that makes all the neighbors fight among themselves for generations.

I think the best way is for the city council to administer it, and for the city council to be the one to maintain the well when it breaks down, to be the one to collect the fees, etc. And that way they save a lot of problems between neighbors and make communities work better. In this case, the auxiliary authority, its function is only to inform the town hall in case the well fails, or there is a water leak in a street, etc.

But in several municipalities, the well or the water issue is still managed by some area or directorate of the city council, such as the "public services" directorate, for example, although I think this complicates the function, since the director changes every three years, and the projects are not given continuity.

But in some more advanced municipalities, they already have a decentralized water and sanitation agency, which makes the drinking water and drainage service of the communities more effective. (later I will talk about decentralized agencies).

QUESTIONS TO REFLECT ON:

In your community, who manages the issue of water?

Do you think that the water service in your community could be improved?

ARE THE AUXILIARY AUTHORITY AND THE CONDOMINIUM PRESIDENT THE SAME?

Currently in Mexico we are having a great growth of condominiums, both vertical and horizontal and mixed, this due to the lack of land and also because every time we want to build places, more closed, with more security, more exclusive, etc.

But normally the auxiliary authority and the president of the board of directors of a condominium, although their functions seem similar, in reality they are different, since the auxiliary authority of a community manages the problems of the street, (what is outside the condominium) that is property of the municipality, and manages it before the same city council, and the president of the condominium, manages before his neighbors the problem of the street or streets that are within his condominium.

Although the president of the condominium can also manage what is outside of his condominium, in case the auxiliary authority ignores it.

And in the case of the condominium, they are governed by the condominium law in force in their state, but they must also obey the municipal edict of their municipality.

And in the case of the auxiliary authority, its functions are based on the municipal organic law of its state, also on the municipal decree that corresponds to it, but it does not have to be based on the condominium law.

The president of the board of directors is elected by the neighbors of his condominium, and the auxiliary authority is elected by the neighbors, but from the entire community.

The president of the board of directors is appointed by the neighbors, and the auxiliary authority is appointed by the city council in turn.

This topic is a bit complicated, but well, it gives me reason to write my experiences that I have had for many years also as president of a homeowner's association in another exclusive book on this particular topic.

QUESTIONS TO REFLECT ON:

Do you live in a subdivision, condominium or other?

Do you know the condominium law of your state?

Do you know the functions of the ejido commissioner?

WHAT ARE DECENTRALIZED PUBLIC BODIES?

Decentralized public bodies to explain it in a simple way and without much fuss, it is an organization that is from the public sector, they have their own legal personality and assets, this means that (it is not a business of someone in particular), they are autonomous (They seek their own money to continue with their function, but if they have to seek to have some form of income to be able to carry out their function for which it was created, which is normally to promote and guarantee social welfare and the development of the community.
In the city councils there are several decentralized public bodies, and with different names and functions, because each city council can create the bodies it requires, but here I give you some examples of them:

There is a decentralized public body that is dedicated to the issue of water, in some municipalities that already have this decentralized public body, they call it ODAPAS, in others they call it in different ways, but in general its function is that you have to pay them annually. or bimonthly, (they may or may not have a meter to charge you), you go to an independent office of the town hall, and in exchange for that contribution, they are in charge of maintaining your municipality's well, of taking care that there are no water leaks throughout the network that takes the water to your home, they have the necessary personnel to go and repair the reported leaks at the required time, and they are monitoring that the water is of quality, they repair the pumps, the pichanchas, etc. All this has a cost, and that is why we must pay for the water that reaches our homes.

I like this topic a lot, because it is really very important, since we are more and more people, and we use a lot of water and waste it a lot, I don't remember the exact figure, but they said that 100% of the water that is extracted from the well for take it to your house, approximately 40% is lost in leaks, and those water leaks were caused by the classic dripping faucet, and the toad in the toilet, I remember that an unrepaired toad can waste up to 200 water tanks a year. (Imagine if each house wastes 200 water tanks per year for each bathroom it has, there are houses with up to 2 bathrooms or more)

Currently we see in the news, that there are places with extreme drought, that there is no water in many parts of the world, even in our beloved Mexico we are already beginning to have problems of water scarcity in some states, that is why I think it is important that there are organisms decentralized public bodies in each of the municipalities, it really is very important, and not just leave this issue to a "neighborhood committee" that apart from them have no experience or knowledge on the water issue, and also do not have time to be checking those things .

On some occasion I proposed to a municipal president that he create a decentralized public body for water and sanitation in that municipality, and he told me that it would be a good idea, but that it would be better not to do it, because it would hit him politically speaking.
Another example of a decentralized public body is what we know as "DIF", which means comprehensive development of the family, this body also has a great job to do within society.

They are in charge of supporting people in a situation of vulnerability, also of supporting family integration, since currently with the rhythm of life that we lead throughout the world, families have been disintegrated, (each one in their own way), they promote social assistance, because every family in every municipality, and in every neighborhood we have our own problems, (and it's not that I don't know that we all have problems), I mean really serious problems (because already being an auxiliary authority) , I saw a lot of very difficult situations that my neighbors faced, and for that reason I informed them of all the good things in which the municipal DIF of my municipality could support them.

For example, the municipal DIF supports people free of charge on issues of:
- Legal advice
- Medical care
- Preventive campaigns (addictions, cancer, suicides, etc.)
- Food assistance
- Etc...

QUESTIONS TO REFLECT ON:

Do you think that in each municipality there should be a body that formally regulates water, to prevent the vital liquid from being wasted?

Do you think that the issue of water should be related to politics or apart from it?

Did you know what the municipal DIF is for?

Do you think there is a need to spread more about the benefits and support granted by the DIF?

WITH WHAT AREAS OR DIRECTIONS IS AN AUXILIARY AUTHORITY RELATED?

During my management as a municipal delegate or auxiliary authority, I was related to different areas, for example:

- Public Safety and Roads
- Urban Development
- Public Works
- Environment
- Public services
- Economic development
- Civil protection
- Physical culture and sport
- Education
- Culture, Tourism, Craft Promotion
- There are some other addresses, and the name may vary (depending on each municipality).

And from each of these areas, I learned many things, but let me comment and share briefly and with all due respect (with no desire to offend anyone), some experiences on the subject of:

When I passed near some element of the police that was on their patrol, I complained that they always passed by, and I saw them sleeping, as an auxiliary authority I found out that they had a 24-by-24 shift, this meant that they worked 24 hours and they rested 24 hours, but obviously when they got home with their family like every human being, they had to repair the lamp that the woman had told them about last week, they had to play with their children, they had to go buy the things they were missing, they had to do a lot of things, and it is clear that they did not sleep the 24 hours they had to sleep, for that reason is that at work they fell asleep as long as they could.

As a graduate in administration, I learned that employees cannot work more than 8 hours, because after that time the body no longer works the same, even now some companies are putting shorter hours or only working four days a week, to achieve that people can enjoy more and be more productive. (I don't know who invented that 24-hour thing for the police) I also found out that their patrols failed their brakes, or they didn't bring good tires and they sometimes have to buy them, or that the guns were no longer useful, or that many times they didn't bring bullets because they charge for each bullet, or if they break a patrol windshield, they have to pay, etc...

Another very interesting thing that I learned is that the homeless are on the loose in the street because they have nowhere to take them, and if they commit an offense, the conciliatory judge does nothing to them, and the patrolmen don't even take them anymore because they know they will return them.

And although the DIF (Comprehensive Family Development) is an auxiliary body to the city council, where they should be supported, the truth is that we see more and more people living on the streets, and this issue has not been resolved as it should.

(So we have a lot of homeless people scaring people away, or having administrative offenses and nothing happens, I think it's an issue that needs to be legislated and soon).
That was how I began to understand why we were wrong in that area, for example, and I began to manage so that many of those things that I saw wrong would be corrected little by little.

I also discovered that there were a lot of police officers, (each one with their telephone number) the federal, the state, the municipal, the state transit, the municipal transit, the bank (in the streets except in the bank), single command, preventive police, ministerial police, national guard, military police, CUSAEM, gender police, neighborhood police, private police, etc. And the functions that each of them performed... (although to be honest and with all due respect, not even they are very clear).

Another situation that I faced is that some neighbors called me very upset, and told me to call the traffic, and to do something with the people who parked in front of their houses, when they went to mass, and it was where I realized that many churches in Mexico do not have parking like in other countries, and this is something that has not been regulated, and at least in my community it caused a lot of trouble.

Something that I also learned was that people normally do not know the road language, most people do not know the difference and the meaning between the yellow line and the white line of the streets, we believe that painting the curbs yellow is for that the streets look beautiful. Or the color of the arrows, or the shapes and colors of the signs.

Imagine I had a retired neighbor, (who one day of leisure) had the great initiative of painting the corner of the street, (thank you for the intention) and said why do they have to be pedestrian crossing lines? I'm going to paint yellow circles, and so he did and no one said anything to him.
(This is how I think road disorder was born in our country)

Or, for example, one day on a cruise far from my community, the traffic light failed and it was a total mess, there were crashes, rumors, and everything we already know happens when a traffic light fails.
And I went on the third day, and it was still the same, so, although I was not an auxiliary authority in that community, I quickly called the person in charge of repairing the traffic lights, and I told him that the traffic light was not working, and he told me that no one had reported it, and the next day it was working, and the chaos was solved.
Another experience I had was that, in a community close to mine, the train track passed by, but many years ago they had put some (pens), that when the train was going to pass, they were lowered so that the drivers could stop. (like in the movies), but one day I was traveling with a friend in his car, and he went over the tracks very quickly, and I asked him why he didn't notice if the train was coming? get off since before the train comes, but he didn't know that pens hadn't been used for a long time.

And when he found out that the pens didn't work, he told me, how is it possible that they don't work, that's very dangerous?

It was at that moment when I told him that this is the reality in our country, but that he could contribute to improving his environment, and go personally to see the delegate of his community so that they could see what could be done to repair them, or put in another system. to alert drivers that the train is coming and thus avoid any possible accident.

That's where you realize that, with just advice or a call to the right person, many problems or accidents in society can be avoided, but in the end we all passed by and complained, but nobody did anything.

Another thing that happened to me is that a car at night did not have its rear lights, and another car hit it slightly when it reached the traffic light, and the neighbors argued about who was to blame.

I remember that my uncle used to tell me that a few years ago, the traffic police used to give you a ticket for not having the lights on your car at 100%, and the truth is that today I have not seen you get a ticket for these reasons, now the cars and buses even bring the lights as if it were a disco and nobody says anything to them.

Currently there are still many things to correct in the area of public and road safety, but together and with the participation of all the auxiliary authorities, each one from their community, over time we will see better results and better communities.

Do you think it is the responsibility of the citizen to report these failures of the train pens?

Do you think it is the responsibility of the city council to be aware and that this does not happen?

Do you think it is the responsibility of both, but many times you do not know where to report or with whom?

Have you been cited for not having a working car light?

Do you think that security is really effective when police officers work 24 hours straight and rest another 24?

One of the many things I learned was that land always has land uses, that there is intensity, density and permitted heights, something that the entire population normally ignores, and this serves so that your neighbor does not put a club on you, or that They build you a 10-story building, where only two levels can be built, or they build 20 little houses on a tiny piece of land, etc...

Another thing that caught my attention and this I have seen at a national level, is that the issue of sidewalks (where there are any), is quite a conflict, because on the one hand the city council tells you that the sidewalks are not yours , but it tells you that you should sweep and clean them, but if it is damaged you should repair it. So, people I think we are very confused regarding this particular topic

Another very interesting thing that I learned is that people always requested speed bumps in front of their houses, arguing that everyone speeds. but the strange thing is that I never saw a neighbor commit a police violation for going too fast. of speed, because there are no traffic patrols in each neighborhood, and the municipal ones that come through are not empowered to infringe, nor did I see maximum speed signs, but I thought, it is useless to put up signs if in the end there is no one who infringe them.

And that's why almost all of Mexico is full of speed bumps in almost all neighborhoods, and the most surprising thing is that people build them overnight, suddenly speed bumps appear where there were none. (and sometimes they are fences that ruin your car from the bottom and nobody is responsible).

But I also learned that in Mexico there is a NOM that says what measures and how a ceiling should be built, but almost nobody knows about it, not even the people from the city council.

Another very important thing that I learned in this area was the advertising that people place on poles, normally many companies, businesses, changarros, etc., put advertising on poles in all neighborhoods, and after a while they are all broken, the poles rusty (because of the wire they put on them), and apart from generating a lot of garbage daily, they generate visual pollution, but many people do not know that this is prohibited, and they continue to do so because there is no one who violates them .

QUESTIONS TO REFLECT ON:

Has it happened to you that suddenly you are driving down a street, and the next day you pass there is already a huge stop?

Do you think the sidewalks in front of your house are owned by the council, or not?

Do you think the council is responsible for sweeping and repairing damaged sidewalks?

In this area I also learned quite a few things, since the streets of my community had already been built for a long time, and therefore they already had many potholes, and as an auxiliary authority I managed the "Re folded" (I don't really know the right word) of the streets, and after For a while, I managed to get almost all the streets in my community re-carpeted, only one street was missing because a neighbor did not want to, until all the drainage was charged beforehand.
And talking to one of the people in charge of the streets, he told me that normally the well-cared-for asphalt of a street lasts about 15 or 20 years.

To which I asked him, what is well-cared-for asphalt? He replied that asphalt is an organic material, and like everything organic over time, the sun, the water, the dust, the weight of the trucks, is deteriorating.

I still did not understand, since any street in any country, even if they are made of cement or asphalt, is exposed to the sun, dust, rain, etc. And at that moment some streets (of asphalt in the United States) came to my mind, which I visited, and they were not at all similar.
I asked him, what is the difference between the asphalt of the United States and the Mexican? He replied that there is none, that the two asphalts are the same and are applied in the same way.

So why are our streets horrible and theirs are often beautiful, I wondered?

He answered me, because the gringos have two drains, one for rainwater and the other for sewage, so in the rainy season and even if the rainwater drains overflow, it is still rainwater, (clean water), on the other hand in Mexico, the drainage overflows because it brings the sewage and rainwater together, and all the chemicals that come out are the ones that damage the pavement the most, and another difference is the thickness of the street, which In the United States they do it according to the regulations and many times here, they only add a bit of asphalt to make it look nice.

Another thing I learned, and I liked it a lot, is that in a street near my community they were putting cobblestone, instead of asphalt or cement, since according to them (it was more traditional and according to the guidelines of the magical town), and also the water is filtered, it helps the subsoil, was what those who built it told me.

And I told the man that what I was supposed to learn as an auxiliary authority, when we repaved our streets in the community, was that before laying the asphalt or laying the cobblestone they must compact very hard so that the water does not filter, and do not do the holes? So, if you compact before the paver, even though the paver absorbs the water, it will stagnate and that causes the water to accumulate under the paver, and it deteriorates faster, and therefore the street disintegrates faster.

He replied that this is the business, and it is a way of always having streets to repair.

Do you think that the streets in Mexico are really well done?

Did you know that, in Mexico, the rain and sewage drainage in almost all municipalities is the same?

Do you think it is ethical, to build a cobblestone street knowing that what they do will not work, and sooner or later they will have to repair it again?

I learned to know the types of trees that could be planted in parks, in forests, in houses, since, for example; A neighbor planted a very pretty little palm tree in her house, and over the years it was a super palm tree, which was destroying the foundations of her house, and it cost her a fortune to throw it away because it was huge.

Because there are really no courses and no one teaches you about the types of trees that we can plant in parks, in houses, etc.

I remember a time, there was a campaign on television where they told you to plant a tree with your parents, and everyone went to the park in my community and planted one, and everyone planted the one they liked or the one they were given, but with Over time they forgot about it, and this became a problem, because there were trees that shed many leaves, and that covered the drains during the rainy season. Others dried up and looked horrible, others grew all crooked, others grew so much that the light from the public lighting was no longer visible and this caused it to look very dark and dangerous at night.

And then we had a big problem, because several of those trees that were planted on the edge of the street, the roots over the years, began to destroy and clog the drains, and then they had to cut down the trees that were huge and precious, regardless it was a pretty penny and very dangerous.

Do you know what kind of trees you can plant in your community park?

Do you know what types of pests can attack the trees in your community?

Should the trees on the sidewalk be cared for by you, or by the town hall?

NOTE: In many places in Mexico, we still have these doubts, although it seems incredible.

I learned where all the garbage generated by my community was going to end up, and the truth was impressive to see how much garbage arrived at that place, how bad it smelled and that we did not have the culture of separating garbage, etc.

Something that caught my attention is that in that year in which I entered as auxiliary authority, the municipal president of my municipality, imposed for the first time, the separation of organic and inorganic garbage, he even ordered the purchase of garbage trucks, with his garbage separator, but the following year, the new president removed that rule, and returned it to how it was before.

That's where I realized that decisions in our country are decided every three years without giving it continuity, the truth is that I think it was a very good initiative to start separating the garbage, in addition to the fact that we had already become accustomed as neighbors to separating it.

Also of the many things I learned, it was that the public lighting was not placed by CFE, that they are only responsible for generating electricity, so that it turns on the lamp outside your house, but that the city council is the one that corresponds to place it or repair it, and that we CFE in our electricity bill charge us the D.A.P which is 10% of your energy consumption, and apart from the City Council they also charge the same amount for generating energy, although no lamp lights in your neighborhood.

Another thing I learned was that this area of the town hall was in charge of cutting the grass in my community park (the truth is that they went every 6 or 8 months to cut it) but then that is why the park was always long and dirty. . Because no one arranged for them to cut it, so the city council was not going to cut it if no one requested it.

QUESTIONS TO REFLECT ON:

In your community, do common areas or parks normally always have uncut grass or litter?

In your community, are the public lighting lamps usually burned out or flickering, and do you know where to report them?

In your community, do you separate organic, inorganic and sanitary waste?

I learned that all businesses had to have their operating license, civil protection permits, the types of business there were, that there were permanent, semi-permanent, established positions, and the regulations that each of them had.

Another thing I learned was how complicated it is for formal businesses to start, although currently they have already tried to regulate it to make it easier, but, even so, I think it is still very complicated and very uneven between formal and informal.

I will tell you about an experience that I had as an auxiliary authority on this topic, and it was that, on the sidewalk in front of the church in my community, there were some commercial premises that were for rent, and an elderly lady wanted to start her own business. tamales to improve their economic situation.

So he ventured out and started his tamale business, for which he had to paint his shop, give his advance payment to the owner, label his sign with the name of the business, get his approvals, request his business operating license from the town hall, put his lowering the commercial light (which is more expensive than the residential one), registering with the hacienda, putting on its gas installation to heat the tamales, putting up some bars for the diners, in short, a series of things to be able to open and comply with everything that is requested of any formal business.

And the lady 15 days after opening, calls me and tells me that she wanted to talk to me, because she had a problem, to which I go and talk to her to find out about her problem and she tells me:
Delegate I was widowed, and I started my business with a lot of sacrifice, and with all my savings, and now a tamale maker is arriving on a tricycle-style bicycle, with his tamales and he stands exactly at the entrance of the church door when mass ends. , and everyone who leaves the church buys from him, for not wanting to cross the street, and apart from that when they finish it they come to leave their garbage in my can. And the man with the tricycle doesn't pay taxes or anything, nor does he have to be here all day. Please help me by reporting it to the town hall, he told me.

As an auxiliary authority, I reported the tamale maker to the corresponding authority of the municipality for 10 consecutive Sundays, and those from the town hall were going to invite in the most decent and formal way that he please leaves because it affected the older lady, to which the tamale maker always ignored.
And one Sunday the police arrived in charge of taking the street vendors away, and all hell broke loose, because some neighbors told me that, because they were taking him away, if he wasn't a thief, that's how they should catch thieves, etc...

I was only doing my job as an auxiliary authority and supporting the old lady's report, then a neighbor told me "#! %" #$%" #$%!" # why are you doing this? And I replied that, just as he had called me to tell me all that that day, he would have called me the previous 10 Sundays to congratulate me on such a decent and formal way of inviting him to retire. And to cut a long story short, after a few months the lady had to close, and lost all her investment.

Do you think the old lady was wrong in not preparing a business plan in the right way?

Do you think the municipal police took too many Sundays to act as they should?

Do you think that I as an auxiliary authority should have ignored and encouraged and let free competition do its job?

It was also very interesting because I remember that I was able to request talks for my community on first aid, preventing fires, etc.

I learned all the operational, financial, etc. problems. faced by firefighters and first responders.
I did not know, for example, that the municipal ambulance paramedics have to pay for all the equipment they carry in their suitcases (which continues to surprise me), the only thing that is not theirs is the ambulances, but the rest they have to pay out of pocket.

Or, for example, firefighters have many shortcomings, and sometimes the firefighter is the same paramedic who performs the two roles of firefighter and paramedic in many municipalities.
In some municipalities in Mexico, they don't even have firefighters, they have to go from other municipalities to help them.

I will tell you about a case in which, in a very distant municipality in the state of Mexico, (I won't say names, so as not to burn), on one occasion there was a fire in a house, and people called 911 and everything was fine, they sent the video, geolocation and everything as if we were in a first world country.

But the reality was that the firefighters arrived two hours later, but the most surprising thing is that they came to put out the fire with "broom sticks", if you read correctly, broom sticks from those branches that cut along the roads, and when they arrived and saw that they could not put out the fire with their super sticks, then the firefighter radioed the base and asked them to send the pipe truck, which took another half hour to arrive, and when the pipe truck arrived, everything was it was burned unfortunately.

And what the firefighter told us is that we shouldn't call 911, because it takes a long time there, so you better call the local emergency number. What if you don't know them, or you're not from that community?

It seems like a funny thing, but it really happened, and it was there that I realized all the shortcomings that we still have as a country.

That is why it is important for us to manage as auxiliary authorities, to improve this 911 system at the national level.

Another thing I learned was that we had a lot of ambulances in the municipality, some from civil protection that belong to the city hall, others from the state government (ISEM), others from the Red Cross, others from the IMSS, others private, and At the end when I asked the people of my community if they knew who to call in case of an emergency, the reality is that hardly anyone knows who to call, many are in poor condition, others do not have gasoline, others do not have brakes and when you need an ambulance (intensive care) there is none.

A friend even told me that when they had an emergency in cdmx, they called an ambulance to the emergency phone number in his community, and it did indeed arrive, and supported the person, but as soon as he recovered they told him, it's $7,000 pesos (it almost goes back to faint).

Another very important thing that I learned in this area was the issue of stray dogs. Suddenly a lot of stray dogs arrived in my neighborhood, and people couldn't even walk anymore, and one of those dogs bit a neighbor, and the neighbor went to report to me that a stray dog had bitten him, but it was a dog that a lady always fed that dog, so we went to see the lady and she said that the dog was not hers, that she was not the owner, who only fed the dogs, (we discovered there why they never left) and the lady did not want to take care of the expenses of the dog bite.

QUESTIONS TO REFLECT ON:

Do you think the lady is right to feed them and that the dogs are still on the street biting people?

Do you think the lady should bring the dogs into her house and take care of them if she loves them so much?

Do you think the city should feed the dogs and give them a home?

On another occasion in the same park in my neighborhood, there was an old lady with her granddaughter in the playground, and suddenly a young man came with a huge black dog (rottweiler), and he was bringing it without a leash, so the dog ran towards the girl, and the girl did not move, she was only scared to see the huge dog and due to that fear it caused a health problem. The young man claimed that the dog had not done anything to the girl, that it only approached him.

QUESTIONS TO REFLECT ON:

Do you think the young man was wrong for not bringing the dog on a leash, even though the dog was very noble and did nothing?

Do you think granny was wrong to take the girl to the playground, and not run to chase the dog away?

Derived from these situations in my neighborhood at that time, I reported and asked the city council for support so that it would be the kennel, and put order in the issue of dogs, and the surprise that I got is that in the municipal edict if it is written that , if someone does not keep their dog on a leash, they are entitled to an infraction, to which I asked them who makes these infractions, because I have never seen anyone who is infracted for not keeping their dog on a leash? which they answered me that, if it is written in the municipal edict, but that there was only one person in charge of doing that in the entire municipality, and that he had a "vochito" from the city council, but that it did not work at that time.

And when I then asked dog control (commonly known as the "perrera") to go after the pack, which had already scared and bitten many people, the city council sent an old truck, with two older men and a lasso, (purely charro style) to capture the dogs, which they never captured and what the gentlemen only told me was, "these dogs are very intelligent, they already know when we are going to come".

In another municipality, I also had to see that the kennel does not even exist, and they have to ask other municipalities for support.

QUESTIONS TO REFLECT ON:

Have you seen someone in your community be infracted for not keeping their pet on a leash, or for not cleaning up their pet's feces?

Is there a kennel in your municipality, and do you know where to request it?

Do you think that people in Mexico lack a lot of culture on the subject of how to care for animals?

In my neighborhood we had a park, and when I was an auxiliary authority, the neighbors at that time told me that in the parks there are always pure courts for men, I asked them what I eat for men?, and they told me yes, that they always The parks' courts are for soccer or basketball, and as women they couldn't play soccer with the men or basketball because they were different forces.
They told me why I didn't manage a volleyball court better, that they could play mixed there, because it was just hitting the ball. (I really found your point of view of the ladies very interesting)

Among the problems that we also had in my community park, and a very important one for being able to play sports, was that of dog poop everywhere, and I'll tell you that on a trip I made to Spain, in one of its parks I saw that they had a bathroom for dogs, if you read correctly "a bathroom for dogs inside the park", which as an auxiliary authority I managed in those years and they just laughed, and they took me crazy.
Another of the procedures that I did and that I saw in a European park, were some tables with their stone chairs, but on the table, they had a chessboard inserted, which I also managed for my community and the result was the same, they told me that hardly anyone knew how to play chess.
Another of the many things that we need and I think is very important is that, in almost no municipality in Mexico, there are public pools, and if there is any pool in your municipality, they are small, they are private and very expensive. (That's why many people don't know how to swim, when it's a super important thing to survive).

Or, for example, I also had the opportunity to see in public schools in other countries, that they have their very cool gymnasiums, even with air conditioning, and just like us they have their physical education subject, but here I remember that they only put us to do gymnastic tables, but we never had a gym in primary or secondary school.
And let's not talk about public golf courses, and many other opportunities to play sports in the United States.

I truly believe that one of the areas where we most need to manage as auxiliary authorities, and to be insisting to our municipal presidents, governors, local and federal deputies, and to anyone who can be asked, is in this sports area, I think that if there were more sports, there would be less crime and less vice.
Although it should be recognized that currently the parks are putting plastic children's games, and some things for skateboards, skates, etc.

QUESTIONS TO REFLECT ON:

Do you think that there are more courts for some other sports in your community or municipality?

Do you think that humans and pets should live in the same area in parks, or should they be different areas?

Do you think that some sports should be exclusive for people with high economic capacity, or should they also be promoted by city councils in communities for all social classes?

As an auxiliary authority I was able to get to know the primary school in my community, I talked with the director and he told me about its shortcomings as a school, within those shortcomings were the police elements when the children left the school, since many times there were suspicious cars at the children go out, I was able to arrange for them to set up a patrol car when the children left school, we put up vertical signs near the school, so that drivers slow down, etc.

I also remember that the director told me that usually during the rainy season the children could not go out for recess due to heavy rains, and they had to put them in a large auditorium so that they could play there without getting wet.

As auxiliary authorities we gave them a "Trampoline" so that the children could have fun inside the auditorium, and get tired jumping.

Also, as an auxiliary authority, you can support the director to negotiate with the local deputy, or the municipal president, some type of help, to improve the facilities or equipment, even request breakfasts.

I remember a trip, that I had the opportunity to attend a public elementary school in the United States and I was impressed with the dining room that the children had, it was incredible, because they passed by a bar and asked for what they wanted for breakfast for free, and in the box with their credential, they were given their cutlery and tray, and they marked with a scanner that they had been given their breakfast, and they had milk and juice refill machines.

It was there that I realized the big difference, since in my elementary school I only had a little store, which sold us pure junk for breakfast.

And that is where you realize the potential you have as an auxiliary authority to manage before the deputies or the municipal president or the president of the republic himself, to one day ensure that our new generations can have that quality of education and facilities.

QUESTIONS TO REFLECT ON:

In the elementary school in your community, do they have a canteen and do they give breakfast to the children?

Does the primary or secondary school in your community have any type of gym or swimming pool?

How do you imagine you could improve education in your community?

In this area, I also learned a lot of things and one of them was when a friend and some guys from abroad came to visit me (because, although many times, we don't believe it, foreigners love Mexico).

But I realized that the City Councils (not all of them, but a large majority) still have a long way to go in terms of tourism, because my friend, for example, wanted to visit museums, and we went, and I realized that museums do not have information in English, and also that in many municipalities there are no museums.

Another thing that happened to me was that, in restaurants, inns, etc. they also don't have a translation on their menus, and the waiters don't have a little course to serve tourists either. (I am talking about municipalities that are not so touristic, but are visited by foreigners)

(something very funny that happened to me was explaining the difference between tostada, sope, taco, flauta, enchilada and chilaquiles).

And to the municipalities that, if they are very touristy, I think that the city council should also give some honesty courses to the businesses, because they see you as a foreigner and want to leave you barefoot the first time you sit down to eat something. (but I clarify, not all are like that)

Another curious thing is that when we were in the car and she saw a sign referring to another population, she asked me how many kilometers away is that place to be able to go and see it? and it was there that I realized that the signs on the roads do not tell you how many kilometers away the next city is. (In some countries they tell you on the road or street signs, the kilometers away from the next city. (I think that advice is very good, because they avoid searching the internet).

Another thing that is very important to improve in this area is the service provided by taxi drivers in the municipalities, since I believe that the municipalities should give them courses in English and customer service, so that they improve the quality of their service, whether for locals or foreigners.

Another thing that I realized, and my dear friend suffered a lot, is that handicrafts (which foreigners love) cannot be transported, because they are very large, or they are very delicate to transport, and nobody He likes that when we get home, we arrive with broken gifts, or that they charge us for luggage.

So, as a suggestion to the artisans, they need to improve the logistics for transportation, because they make very beautiful crafts, but they are very large and foreigners do not fit in their suitcases, or they are very easy to break during transportation.

In terms of culture, in my municipality I realized that there was only one house of culture, despite the fact that we were 53 communities in the entire municipality.

On one of those trips I had the opportunity to be in Spain, and usually in each community, no matter how small it was, they had their culture house, although it was not very big, but the town hall sent them classes in some trade, language etc. In order to improve the quality of life of its inhabitants, which I liked very much, and I tried to manage this as an auxiliary authority, and they told me that there were no resources.

But well, the important thing was to try, and continue managing it so that one day in Mexico, as in that country, each community can have, even if it is a small house of culture, because many times people cannot go to the municipal seat for a course.

Do you think that artisans should adapt to the needs of foreigners, or should foreigners adapt to the crafts made by artisans?

Do you think there should be at least one small culture house in your community?

There are many areas and many things that I learned, and these are just small examples of things that you really learn as an auxiliary authority.

DO I REALLY THINK WE CAN CHANGE MEXICO FOR THE BETTER?

Once a friend told me that I was a dreamer, that Mexico no longer had a solution, that here everyone does what they want and how they want, that it is a town without law, and etc., etc.

Obviously, my friend had never left Mexico and did not know what it is like to live in other countries, she only based her comments on the famous radio corridor, on what she heard out there.
Even when I came back from a trip, he asked me why you always come back so happy, and I answered that when you go on a trip and see those clean streets and beautiful sidewalks, your spirits even rise.

And this person told me, I really don't understand you, how different can the streets be in other countries? What can be different about a street in another country, that the streets of Mexico don't have?
And I answered him only with a smile, and I told him, you have to go to see them, and you will see for yourself and you will understand me.

Later, over time, I had the opportunity to go live and study in Europe, (of course it is beautiful to live there), but like everything in this world, it also has its drawbacks.
Although this book is not to speak ill of anyone, on the contrary, it is to motivate you to participate from your trench, to help improve your community.

But after living in Europe for a while, I remembered a famous phrase that an older friend of the family told me, and he said "we all see the garden in front of us greener, until you are not in it".

And if it is true, we all believe that other countries are the best and Mexico is the worst, but when you live in those countries, you realize and value what you have in yours.
And I began to reflect, what do these countries have that mine cannot have? Or do these Europeans, do they have two heads, or four arms?

The answer was, no, they don't have two heads or four arms, they just had better organization, and they had a vision of where they want to take their communities.
They have nice sidewalks, (we can also build them), they have well-made streets, (we can also do them), they have a well-organized garbage system, (we can also organize ourselves and do it). And so many things that they have very well, and that are not impossible for us Mexicans to do.

But aside from us, we have a lot of advantages, we have an incredible climate, which allows us to go out all year to work, we have super friendly people, we have various types of climates and regions, we have a delicious and varied gastronomy, we have coasts, deserts, forests, etc.
In general, I saw that we had everything to be better, compared to many other countries in the world, we only need to organize ourselves, and (as a good administrator that I am, I realized that we lacked) set a vision and a mission of where we want to go? bring to our communities? How do we want our neighbors and ourselves to live?

In general, I think we need to love our country, for example; We only put up the flag when it's September 15 and just to celebrate, and then we don't have any flags all year.

(In my house, I have a flagpole every day of the year, with my Mexican flag waving, which fills me with great pride) although many neighbors ask me, why do I have it? What if I am a school? And I tell them that this flag represents everything, my country, my family, my friends, my neighbors, my joys and my sorrows, my living and my dead.
And they like what I tell them and in the end they tell me, you're right, I think I'll put mine in my house too.

But going back to the topic, (I got off track a bit), after a while I ran into my friend, and she told me what do you think?, and I asked her what?, she told me that she was remembering me recently, son had already graduated a few years ago and had a good job, and that they had sent him to work in the united states. Then her son supported her so that she could visit him in the United States, and when she saw the streets she remembered me, and she said now I understand my friend because he came back so happy.

She told me, now I understand what you were saying about the difference in the streets, I didn't believe that the sidewalks or the streets could be so different, I was even surprised by how the Americans took care of the plants.
She told me that when she came back she wanted to do the same thing with the plants outside her house, (super pretty decoration) and that when she came back from work, they had already been mistreated.

But I was glad to meet her, and that she told me her experience, because I verified that it is true, that until we see how different it is possible to live, that is when we begin to act on the matter. And when we value what we have as a country.

That is why I believe that yes, that if our country can be improved, but we must share that vision, among the inhabitants of our communities, we must make them see that, if we can live better, that we have everything to achieve it, we just need to work in team, and organized.

Let go of those eternal meals, hasn't it happened to you? That you're at family meals or with friends, and they start with, if "X" party is the good one, or that "Y" candidate is the bad one or the good one, that if he is ugly, that if he is naco, that if he is fat, that if he is drunk, that if he does not know German, etc.

And they are talks where they all end up fighting and thundering even with the girlfriend (it happened to a friend's cousin). And in the end, you don't even know the food, and we still don't solve anything and worst of all, the usual potholes continue, and everything remains the same.

Or there is the one that says "now that I am a millionaire I am going to go live abroad", but the truth from my point of view, like our beautiful and beloved Mexico there are not two. (and they never become millionaires, which is the worst).

Once, a friend also told me that I was wrong, that, if he believed that, just by having pretty sidewalks or pretty streets, we were going to live better? I replied that it is not only having pretty streets and sidewalks, you can also manage the parks, lighting, security, endless things, which can be managed as an auxiliary authority, before the competent authorities, to help improve. But the truth is that, even if you could only walk down a nice sidewalk or street, it changes your mood 100%. (it happened to me)

That is why I believe that despite all the problems that we have as a country, and the crises and everything bad that you want, I believe that together we can get ahead, if each one of us in each neighborhood motivates us to participate as auxiliary authorities, then the sum of all of them, will be the result of a better country.
 Which in the end I think is what we all would like?

Because I have the belief that a country is formed from the small, from below, from the values of each home, plus other homes, they build the neighborhood, and the sum of other neighborhoods builds your municipality, and so the states and so a great country.

Because, even if we have the best president, or the best governor, or the best mayor or municipal president, if the homes or neighborhoods are not doing well, there will be no way to get ahead. (they are not magicians or miraculous) of course it helps a lot, that they are good rulers, but if we help them from below as auxiliary authorities to manage the real needs of our communities, we will advance more, and faster.

I have met several foreigners living in Mexico, and they love
it, for something, don't you think?

But now the question of the $64,000, how do we make it so
that everyone knows and can see a well-made and beautiful
street, a well-made and beautiful sidewalk, efficient public
transportation, first-world public lighting, etc., but not the can
we take everyone abroad to see it and learn about it, and then
they can apply it in their communities?

There are even municipal presidents who have not left their
town, how can we ask for pears from the elm tree?

I had to travel to a municipality, where it is said that the
municipal president painted the garrisons in another color,
because he did not like yellow because it was the color of the
soccer team that he hated.

On another occasion, I was told that a municipal president
ordered the color of all the public lighting posts in his civic
plaza to be changed, because the previous president had put
them in the color of his party, and the new president was from
another party.

In another municipality, I had to see how the president in turn
changed the traffic signs to the color of his party, and not the
one that corresponds to him by official rule.
All this happens, I don't think, because they are bad people,
nor is it about speaking ill of anyone, but because many things
are ignored.

So, I think my answer is that this change has to take place little by little, and if something good and beautiful is done in any community, the neighboring community will copy it (although its leader has not traveled abroad), I could even improve it.

But that's what it's all about, we have to start doing things well done, and efficiently.

QUESTIONNAIRE TO SEE HOW ORGANIZED WE ARE AS A SOCIETY?

The idea of this questionnaire is that you apply it to your relatives, friends, neighbors, etc., to whomever you want, even to yourself, and be really sincere in their answers, and in the end, we will see how well organized we are as a society. in such basic and important things.

1.- Do you know the municipal side of your municipality or mayor's office?

2.- Do you know or do you know who your local deputy is?

3.- Do you know what the function of the aldermen or councilors of your municipality or mayor's office is?

4.- Do you know or do you know who is the auxiliary authority of your community?

5.- Do you know the differences between subdivision, ejido, condominium?

6.- Do you know who is responsible for changing public lighting in your community?

7.- Do you know who is responsible for infracting you if you don't keep your dog on a leash?

8.- What is the color of the inorganic waste container in your municipality?

9.- Do you know the difference between the yellow stripe and the white stripe on the streets of your community?

10.- If you have an emergency, do you know the telephone number of the local police in your municipality?

If you answered "I DON'T KNOW" to at least 5 questions, don't worry, almost the entire country doesn't know the right answers.

For these reasons, they are the ones that we should all get more involved as a society, in order to live together in a correct way, and to be able to reach some day, that almost perfect society to which we aspire.

ABOUT THE AUTHOR

Cosme Santoveña Velázquez, has lived and studied in Mexico and Spain, has a degree in administration from the AUTONOMOUS UNIVERSITY OF THE STATE OF MEXICO, a diploma in finance, and a diploma in Comparative Histories of Development from the MIDE, he was a substitute municipal delegate, owner municipal delegate, he is a businessman, investor, actor, consultant, builder, and is currently the president of a Civil Association of settlers.

Considered by many as "an expert voice on issues related to auxiliary authorities and businesses"

During all these years it has managed and supported thousands of people both in Mexico and abroad, so that in one way or another they improve their quality of life.

Cosme Santoveña currently lives with his two ducks, is single, without children, and spends most of his time trying to improve his environment.

To the English-speaking readers, I want to apologize in advance if some words are not correct, I have used the internet translator, since many words are administrative terms of Mexico.

THANK YOU

HERE YOU CAN WRITE DOWN THE DOUBTS YOU
HAVE, SO YOU CAN ASK
THE AUXILIARY AUTHORITY
OF YOUR COMMUNITY